Table of Contents

Can you find these words?

chrysalis

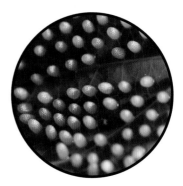

eggs

leaves

nectar

Butterfly

A butterfly is a flying insect.

It tastes plants with its feet!

It lays **eggs** on a tasty plant. Caterpillars hatch from the eggs.

5

A caterpillar eats **leaves**.
It eats and eats.

leaf

It grows and grows!

The caterpillar forms a **chrysalis.**

chrysalis

The chrysalis opens.

A butterfly comes out.
It is time to fly!

It flies to find food.

A butterfly's tongue is like a straw.

nectar

It drinks **nectar** from flowers.

Did you find these words?

The caterpillar forms a **chrysalis**.

It lays **eggs** on a tasty plant.

A caterpillar eats **leaves**.

It drinks **nectar** from flowers.

Photo Glossary

 **chrysalis** (KRIS-uh-lis): A butterfly in a quiet stage between caterpillar and adult, spent inside a hard shell.

 **eggs** (egs): Oval or round objects that contain the babies of insects or other animals.

 **leaves** (leevs): Flat, usually green structures attached to a stem growing from a tree or plant.

 **nectar** (NEK-tur): A sweet liquid from flowers that bees gather and make into honey.

Index

About the Author

R.E. Robertson is an author and nature lover. His favorite pastimes include reading, cooking, camping, and spending time with his wife, children, and grandchildren.

www.rourkeeducationalmedia.com

PHOTO CREDITS: Cover ©Lisa Thornberg; Pg 10, 11 © Liliboas; Pg 2, 13, 14, 15 © biffspandex; Pg 2, 5, 14, 15 © Ismael Montero Verdu; Pg 2, 6, 14, 15 © Perytskyy; Pg 2, 8, 14, 15 © skynetphoto; Pg 3 © VDCM Image; Pg 4 © McKinneMike; Pg 7 © AlasdairJames; Pg 9 © tenra; Pg 12 © Els van der Gun

Edited by: Keli Sipperley
Cover and interior design by: Kathy Walsh

Library of Congress PCN Data
Butterfly / R.E. Robertson
(Flying Insects)
ISBN 978-1-73160-583-2 (hard cover)(alk. paper)
ISBN 978-1-73160-457-6 (soft cover)
ISBN 978-1-73160-636-5 (e-Book)
ISBN 978-1-73160-694-5 (ePub)
Library of Congress Control Number: 2018967328

Printed in the United States of America,
North Mankato, Minnesota